LIGHTNING BOLT BOOKS™

Helicopters
on the Move

Jeffrey Zuehlke

Lerner Publications Company
Minneapolis

For Geoff, my
favorite high-
flying buddy

Lerner Publications Company
A division of Lerner Publishing Group, Inc.
241 First Avenue North
Minneapolis, MN 55401 U.S.A.

Website address: www.lernerbooks.com

Library of Congress Cataloging-in-Publication Data

Zuehlke, Jeffrey, 1968–
      Helicopters on the move / by Jeffrey Zuehlke.
         p.   cm. — (Lightning bolt books™— vroom-vroom)
      Includes index.
      ISBN 978–0–7613–6027–8 (lib. bdg. : alk. paper)
      1. Helicopters—Juvenile literature. I. Title.
   TL716.2.Z8423 2011
   629.133'352—dc22   2010016446

Manufactured in the United States of America
1 — CG — 12/31/10

Contents

Chopper Motion

Whup! Whup! Whup! Whup! Whup!
What is that up in the sky?

It's a helicopter!

Helicopters are amazing aircraft.

What can they do?

This helicopter flies above the mountains.

They can fly high and fast.

Helicopters can also fly low and slow.

This military helicopter flies slowly over a field.

They can hover in one spot in the air.

Hovering helicopters can land in small spaces. This helicopter is landing on a ship.

Helicopters can land almost anywhere. This helicopter is in the desert.

How They Work

How do helicopters fly?
They have special wings called rotary wings.

Rotary wings are long and narrow.

The main rotor turns the rotary wings. The wings spin around fast.

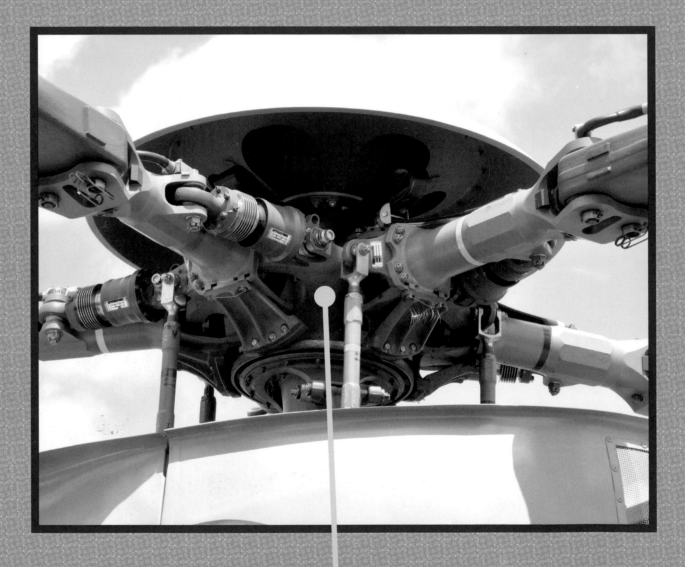

The main rotor is in the center of the wings.

The spinning wings lift the helicopter into the air.

But who flies the helicopter?

Chopper Control

The pilot! The pilot uses controls to fly the helicopter. The controls are in the cockpit.

The cockpit is at the front of the helicopter.

One control is the power lever.
The power lever makes the
helicopter fly up, down, or hover.

This is the
power lever.

This is the stick.
It makes the helicopter move forward, backward, or even sideways!

DANGER→

The tail rotor spins the tail wings. The spinning wings turn the helicopter.

17

The pilot uses
the rudder
pedals to move
the tail rotor.

Helicopter pilots use their
feet to press down on a
helicopter's rudder pedals.

Special Jobs

Helicopters do special jobs.
This helicopter works
for the TV news.

The helicopter flies
slowly over the action.
The cameraperson gets
a good view.

Police officers use helicopters to find suspects.

Suspects are people the police think have broken a law.

This helicopter helped catch a suspect!

STATE TROOPER

Some helicopters work as ambulances. They can get people who are sick or hurt to the hospital fast.

This air ambulance lands on top of a hospital.

23

Helicopters help fight fires.

This helicopter is picking up some water.

Helicopters dump water and chemicals on fires. The water and chemicals help put the fires out.

This helicopter helps fight a forest fire in California.

Rescue helicopters help reach lost or hurt people.

Do you see the person hanging below the helicopter?

The helicopter is lifting
this person to safety.
The helicopter
saved the day!

Helicopter Diagram

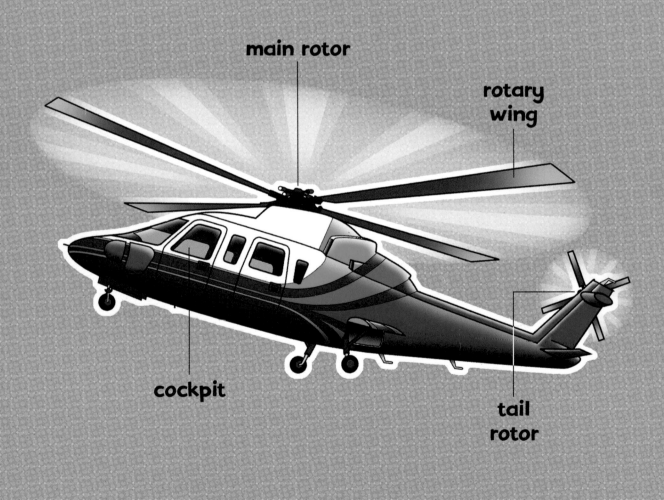

main rotor

rotary wing

cockpit

tail rotor

Fun Facts

- In 1483, an Italian inventor named Leonardo da Vinci came up with an idea for a helicopter. He drew a picture of the machine, but he never tried to build it.

- Helicopters have many names. They are called rotorcraft, choppers, whirlybirds, and eggbeaters.

- The fastest helicopter is the Westland Lynx. It can fly 249 miles (401 kilometers) per hour. A car on a highway moves at about 60 miles (97 km) an hour.

- Large helicopters have two main rotors but no tail rotor. The main rotors work together to turn the helicopter and help it carry heavy loads.

Glossary

aircraft: a machine that can fly through the air

cockpit: the place where the pilot sits

hover: to stay in one spot in the air

main rotor: the part of a helicopter that spins the rotary wings

power lever: a lever that makes a helicopter go up, down, or hover

rotary wings: the wings on a helicopter

rudder pedals: pedals that move the tail rotor

stick: a lever that makes a helicopter go forward, backward, or sideways

tail rotor: a part that spins the tail wings

Further Reading

Boeing Kids' Page: Let's Fly!
http://www.boeing.com/companyoffices/aboutus/kids

Brecke, Nicole, and Patricia M. Stockland. *Airplanes and Ships You Can Draw.* Minneapolis: Millbrook Press, 2010.

Hanson, Anders. *Let's Go by Helicopter.* Edina, MN: Abdo, 2008.

Lindeen, Mary. *Helicopters.* Minneapolis: Bellwether Media, 2008.

Robin Whirlybird on Her Rotorcraft Adventures
http://rotored.arc.nasa.gov

Index

Photo Acknowledgments

The images in this book are used with the permission of: © Stacy Barnett/Dreamstime.com, p. 1; U.S. Navy photo by Mass Communication Specialist 2nd Class Daniel Barker/Released, p. 2; © Francesco Vaninetti/Dreamstime.com, p. 4; U.S. Navy photo by Mass Communication Specialist 2nd Class Shannon Renfroe/Released, p. 5; © Aurora Open/SuperStock, p. 6; AP Photo/U.S. Air Force, Andy M. Kin, p. 7; © Michel Cramer/Dreamstime.com, p. 8; U.S. Navy photo/Released, p. 9; © Science Faction/SuperStock, p. 10; © Patrick Allen/Dreamstime.com, p. 11; © Thomas Dutour/Dreamstime.com, p. 12; © Transtock/SuperStock, pp. 13, 18; © IndexStock/SuperStock, p. 14; © iStockphoto.com/Mutlu Kurtbas, p. 15; © Thor Jorgen Udvang/Dreamstime.com, p. 16; © David Gowans/Alamy, p. 17; © Chuck Mason/Alamy, p. 19; © Novastock/Stock Connection Blue/Alamy, p. 20; © Pikes Peak International Hill Climb/Artemis Images, p. 21; © Larry Mulvehill/CORBIS, p. 22; © Medicimage Ltd./Visuals Unlimited, Inc., p. 23; © Sardegna/La Presse/ZUMA Press, pp. 24, 25; © Ashley Cooper Pics/Alamy, pp. 26, 27; © Laura Westlund/Independent Picture Service, p. 28; © Ivan Cholakov/Dreamstime.com, p. 29; © Serjm/Dreamstime.com, p. 30; © Mark Simms/Dreamstime.com, p. 31.

Front cover: © Ramon Berk/Dreamstime.com (top); © Stasvolik/Dreamstime.com (bottom).